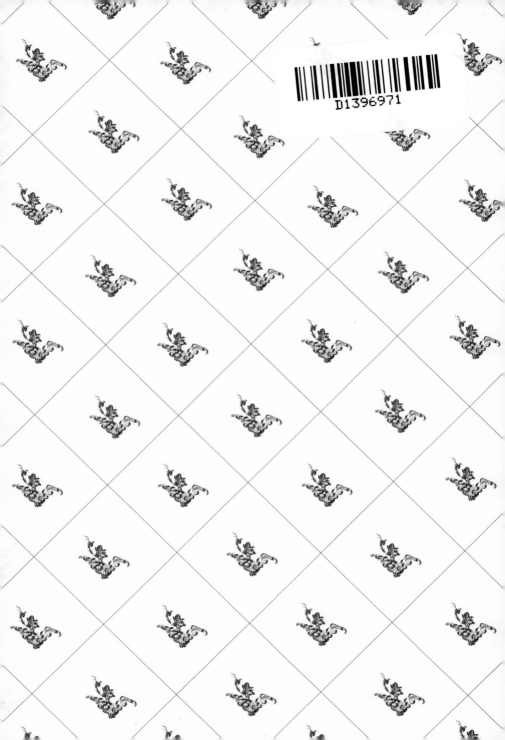

In the
Growing
Places

Rita J. Maggart

In the Growing Places

Written and Illustrated by
Rita J. Maggart

PROVIDENCE HOUSE PUBLISHERS
Franklin, Tennessee

Printed in the United States of America

00 99 98 97 96   5 4 3 2 1

Library of Congress Catalog Card Number: 96-69159

ISBN: 1-881576-96-5

Unless otherwise noted, all scripture is taken from *The New American Standard Bible* (R), © The Lockman Foundation 1960, 1962, 1963, 1968, 1971, 1972, 1973, 1975, 1977. Used by permission.

Scripture quotations marked (TLB) are taken from *The Living Bible* copyright © 1971. Used by permission of Tyndale House Publishers, Inc., Wheaton, Illinois 60189. All rights reserved.

Cover design by Susan Hulme. Front cover photograph by Dennis Wile. Back cover photograph by Rich Mays.

PROVIDENCE HOUSE PUBLISHERS
238 Seaboard Lane • Franklin, Tennessee 37067
800-321-5692

*T*o my Mother and Father
who always encouraged me.

Contents

# Preface

My Dear Lord,

Becoming a published writer has seemed a lot like cleaning out closets. No one, except me, can make the decisions of what to keep and what to toss. The day finally comes to sort through years of accumulated clutter so that the admonition in *Disciplines of the Beautiful Woman* by Anne Ortlund to "Eliminate and Concentrate" becomes a reality.

You know how every writer dreams of being read—that is because a writer by nature is also a reader—a collector of words. My collections are in the form of journal writings, notes taken while reading, and a collection of quotes.

With these collections and with guidance from You, what's in my mind to tell, and in my heart to draw, and in my hands to create can, and will be, brought together in a unified, coherent work which will allow me to *communicate and create.*

But, first, I must know my mission. Why is it that I must communicate and create? What is this message that You have reserved for me alone to tell? Who will You bring into my life to help make my passion become reality?

My mission and its message is this:

To visually explain through arranging flowers Your most
profound message: "It took death to come alive." Just as the
arranger cuts the flower, cleans and prepares it to make it
ready for service, then strategically places it ever so gently
so that its beauty can be seen, so too will You become the
artist in my life when I become like the yielding flower. In
the hands of the artist, the life of the flower begins with its
death, just as my life begins with my death to self.

Why must I communicate and create?

The passion is real—to give to others the healing tools You
have given me. Journal writing is a healing tool. Flower
arranging is a healing tool. Drawing is a healing tool. I have
not owned what I have not given away.

Who will You send to assist me?

Already, You have sent many to help me, and I am excited
because I know You will allow me to meet others. The
opportunities You have given me and the "angels unaware"
who have entered my life could only have been provided by
a God who is directing my steps as I succeed and fail as
Your trustworthy servant.

I know there is a personal mission inside me.

And, I know that even through my *"Lines of Confusion"*
there is a sense of order that You see clearly. As I clean

out this closet and sort out the clutter, there is a peace that comes in knowing that, in Your perfect plan, the mission will be complete. "Eliminate and Concentrate," stated another way in Jeremiah 15:19, applies to me: "If you extract the precious from the worthless, you will become my spokesman."

· O ·

Throughout this book I have signed each letter with the symbol [· O ·]. This is a secret symbol we use in our family to send the message *I Love You.*

$\mathcal{A}$cknowledgments

I refer to the people I must thank for their assistance in making this book a reality as my "angels unaware." I don't believe any of the following "angels" could have possibly known the impact each would have on my life as our lives crossed in providence:

My mentor, teacher, and friend Joseph E. Smith introduced me to this world of beauty. Jan and Phil Sutton opened their home and hearts and taught me most of what I know about flower arranging. Sheila Macqueen taught me the art of English flower arranging, and Martha Kesler taught me the beauty of Ikebana. I wish to thank my sister Joyce Wrye and sister-in-law Martha Funke who are both natural artists; my mother-in-law Mildred Maggart who generously shares with me the beauty in her home and her years of experience in flower arranging; my spiritual mothers Caroline Stevens, Peggy Phillips, Emma Thompson, and Harriett Thompson who were my Bible teachers in my infant years; and my friends Cathye Hancock, Trisha Peek, Laverne Sutton, Jean Davis, Rosemary Paschall, Lisa Kennedy, Lois Sugar, and Van Breast who shared with me their art of encouragement.

Those who read and critiqued my manuscript were Ginny Elder, Lucinda Hall, Melinda Sparks, Shelley Averbuch, Sue Johnson, Susanna Clark, and Pam Eskew. Their input was invaluable and I deeply appreciate their efforts.

To Jim Wheeler and James Nihan, thanks for helping me
cultivate a beautiful growing place to share and enjoy.

Many thanks to Porter Crutchfield who has been my loyal
friend for twenty years and who takes care of my family
while I am off being creative. Daisy King introduced me to
Providence House Publishers who took me into their family
of authors and brought to life my journals of the past
seventeen years.

Thanks also to Mary Bray Wheeler, Jo Jaworski, Judy
Coursey, and my publisher Andy Miller who first said my
drawings could be used. To all at Providence House: "Your
Name Is 'Providence,' too!"

Sometimes we encounter an "angel unaware" who is
beyond comprehension. In my case, he was Chuck Cooper.
From scraps of paper with handwritten journal entries,
Chuck used the miracle of modern technology to edit my
words and put them into a computer. With Chuck's help I
began to see the reality of IN THE GROWING PLACES.

Madeleine L'Engle said, "When the words mean even more
than the writer knew they meant, then the writer has been
listening." The author Sarah Hornsby has been listening.
Thanks to her devotional book, *The Fruit of the Spirit*, I have
had a walk with wisdom for the past eight years.

And finally, I thank my husband John, who loves me with his
arms wide open, and our three sons Brad, Bill, and Stephen,
who had to move over and "Make Room for Mama."

In the Growing Places

My Dear Lord,

I am writing this book, Lord,
because You have answered my prayer
to keep me
in the growing places.

Always, always, I must communicate and create.

This writing is for all those times I
have failed to communicate and create.
The missed opportunities.
The times I was intimidated
or simply didn't see the potential
to glorify You through my art.

This book is an offering and an attempt
to stay
in the growing places.

· O ·
Rita

Calling My Name

My Dear Lord,

Here I am at the crossroads, Lord,
looking for direction.

I say I'm Your servant,
but I will not take
the first step
toward servitude.

It is so hard to say:
"I will follow You,
just lead."

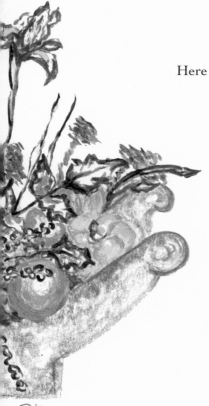

Here I am at the crossroads, Lord,
looking for direction.
You stand here boldly,
I stand here lame.
You stand here gently,
Calling my name.

· O ·

Today if you hear His voice,
Do not harden your hearts.
—Hebrews 4:7

Rita

Encourager and Critic

My Dear Lord,

To feel successful in my art, I need both of
these people:

The Encourager
and
The Critic.

The Encourager will express support for my
work and will be there when I need to feel worthy
of my calling.

The Critic will help me balance my enthusiasm
with objectivity and will give me valuable words
that will, when heeded, make me better.

I pray, Lord, with your help, sometime during my life
I will find that rare individual who will be both
encourager and critic!

· O ·

Something Beautiful for God

My Dear Lord,

Please teach me

To Be
Something Beautiful for God

To Create
Something Beautiful for God

To Share
Something Beautiful for God

You, Lord, have created me,
You have given me these gifts.
You have loved me enough
To open doors of opportunity
To share Your gifts.

Help me now as I strive
To Be,
To Create,
To Share
Something Beautiful for God.

· O ·

*To show great love for God and our
neighbor we need not do great things. It is
how much love we put in the doing that
makes our offering
Something Beautiful for God.*

—Mother Teresa

Before honor comes *humility.*
—Proverbs 15:33

Only After

My Dear Lord,

How do I become what You want me to be?
    The key is not in the efforts I make to improve myself,
    The key is in the efforts I make to improve others.

Success comes
    only after
        I've helped make someone else successful.

Honor comes
    only after
        I have helped make others better than myself.

Love comes
    only after
        I have given away more than I need to receive.

Forgiveness comes
    only after
        I have forgiven others.

Life comes
    only after
        I am willing to die to self.

· O ·

eally Me

My Dear Lord,

It's wonderful to see the beauty of my child,
the joyful moments in his life
and the excitement received from success.

But —

There are other times in my child's life
when he is not so pleasant and
when he reflects what he has experienced from me:
the Sharp Words,
the Quick Temper,
and
the Selfishness.

Thank you, dear Lord, for the teachers of my children
who reveal to me these
Unflattering Traits
and
help me to see
that the one they were speaking of was
really me.

· O ·

Moment in Time

My Dear Lord,

Edgar Allen Poe spoke of poems as things which give "momentary pleasure," the goal of which is not necessarily truth.

I find this "momentary pleasure" in the art of flower arranging. I look at Your beauty in nature and I marvel. I look closely at the flower and discover a new color or form or intricacy that I had never seen before.

Thank you, Lord, for teaching me how to enjoy these flowers at their peak of beauty for my "momentary pleasure" in their *moment in time.*

· O ·

You and Me, Lord

My Dear Lord,

Mothers are full of advice.
Fathers are full of correction.
Siblings are full of fight.
Teachers are full of facts.
Preachers are full of quotes.

I'm not sure there is anyone
I want to be around. I
guess that just leaves
You and Me, Lord.

· O ·

The Trash Before the Treasure

My Dear Lord,

You are teaching me that the only valuable art is the art I throw away. I have read that if you must frame every painting or publish every book, you will never reach the highest level of creativity.

Allow me the freedom to let go of pages and pages of words and sheet after sheet of drawings. They are only *the trash before the treasure.*

· O ·

Townes Van Zandt, a songwriter, wrote
"Where you've been is good and gone; all you keep
is the getting there."

Your Joy May Be Made Full

My Dear Lord,

You speak to me
in silence, Lord, and
Your plans are revealed
to me through prayer.

I am slow to hear
because of the clutter
and confusion in my
life, but You call me into
Your sanctuary and You
speak to me.

The joy is overwhelming when I let go of
my own desires and replace them with
Your desires! What relief is felt when
the last finger is removed from my
tight clutch on the world!

Now, Your joy and my joy
can be made the same as I
ponder on Your words in
John 15:11: "These
things I have spoken to
you, that My joy may
be in you, and *that*
your joy may be
made full."

· O ·

Belonging to You

My Dear Lord,

*"The farther behind I leave the past, the closer I am
to forging my own character."*
—*Isabelle Eberhardt*

You know my past,
and You
know my pain.
In You, Lord,
I begin and continue
to heal and grow.

With your help, I
am forging
my own character and
becoming the
woman you would have
me become.

I love you, Lord, and
I love the hope
that comes from
belonging to You.

· O ·

 An Empty Person

My Dear Lord,

Empty people speak empty words.

When I study, when I think,
when I fill myself with Your words,
then I can begin to give away
the gift of wisdom.

Stay with me, Lord,
in these pondering moments
that
my thoughts
may be
Your thoughts
and that
my deeds
may be
Your deeds.

Help me guard against
the luxury
of being
an empty person

· O ·

Mary treasured up all these things,
pondering them in her heart.
—Luke 2:19

Pray Before I Speak

My Dear Lord,

If I would pray before I speak,
just think how much wiser
I would sound!

Lord, I am your mouthpiece in
guiding my children. Please give
me Your wisdom and not my
selfish thoughts. Let my children
always know that it is through
love that they are rebuked and
corrected. Shed light on my
face and peace in my heart
as I speak so that Your
glory is visible.

Help my children to know that an
over-abundance of love comes from me
and that an infinite world of wisdom
comes from You. Remind me each day
that I should *pray before I speak.*

· O ·

*She opens her mouth in wisdom, and the
teaching of kindness is on her tongue.*
—*Proverbs 31:26*

Straight is the line of duty,
Curved is the line of beauty.
—William Hogarth

The Interruptions

My Dear Lord,

My life is a series of interruptions. I can never seem to accomplish anything because I am always responding, knocking down one crisis after another, never staying very long in any one place.

Why can't I tolerate interruptions? I keep waiting for that one big block of uninterrupted time to start on a project, such as sewing, or cleaning closets, or reading a book. But, of course, it never comes.

Help me, dear Lord, to know that I can function with interruptions, and teach me not to use them as an excuse for wasting time. Here I am, Lord, willing to serve You, even through *the interruptions*.

· O ·

Manually Competent

My Dear Lord,

Sofu Teshigahara, the founder and headmaster of the Sogetsu school of flower arranging, has written:

> There are three categories into one of which any artist can be placed. These are: Manually Competent, Outstanding and Original, and, finally, Genius. When one is learning an art, it is an extremely difficult task to attain even the first of these stages.

Why, Lord, do I want to skip all the early stages and go straight to "genius"? I make life very difficult by judging myself too soon. Remind me that I learn best from my mistakes. Teach me to allow myself all the necessary steps to become *manually competent*.

· O ·

In Silence

My Dear Lord,

In silence answers are found.
In silence peace is felt.
In silence creativity is sparked.
In silence energy is renewed.
In silence thoughts are released.
In silence the mind is cleared.
In silence gentleness is restored.
In silence self-worth is established.
In silence the body is healed.
In silence the hearing is keened.
In silence I talk with God.
In silence I am one with myself.

In my quiet moments with You the answers come.
Please help me to remember that prayer begins in
silence. Still my mind and my body that I might truly
listen and receive Your wisdom. Only when I become
an open vessel for Your thoughts do I feel the peace
that comes from being *in silence* with You.

· O ·

*Silence is the element in which great
things fashion themselves.
— Thomas Carlyle*

Rita

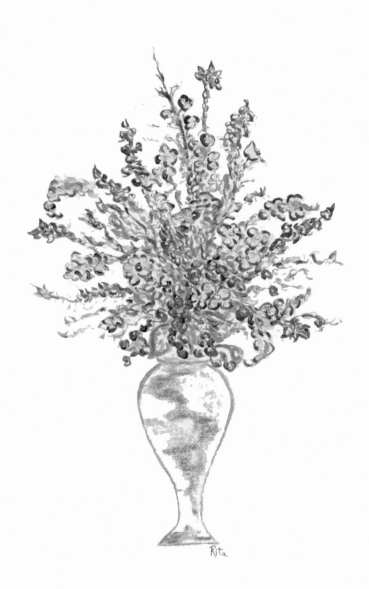

Listening Is Learning

My Dear Lord,

I remember asking my children when they were little:
"Do you know why God gave you two ears and only
one mouth?"

They knew this was a trick question, so they really
didn't want to answer. But, I answered it for them
anyway: "God gave you two ears and one mouth
because He wants you to listen twice as much as
you speak."

Lord, you have taught me there are two things that I
cannot do and speak at the same time: one is to write;
the other is to listen. Lord, help me to be a listener,
because:

> Writing is listening
> and
> *Listening is learning.*

· O ·

Work of Art

My Dear Lord,

The beauty of flowers on this earth is certainly one of Your greatest gifts to mankind.

Today, I discovered another purpose for Your gift of flowers. In my search for unusual containers, I occasionally will sniff out a promising garage sale. During my most recent outing, I found a somewhat valuable vase that had obviously been broken. Someone had lovingly glued it back together in several places.

The vase had lost its appeal as a decorative piece of art, but had gained status as a wonderful container for flowers. With an abundance of blooms overflowing its edges, the cracks and chips disappeared and the formerly broken vessel took on new life.

What a lesson I learned! Flowers transformed the vase into a truly beautiful and useful *work of art*.

Lord, please transform me, too.

· O ·

Enjoy the Process

My Dear Lord,

The everyday art of flower arranging is the perfect medium for someone who does not believe that he/she is a "natural" artist.

There are three reasons why I am inspired to arrange flowers:

The FLOWERS may yearn to be picked and brought into my home to share their wonderful beauty with family and friends.

The CONTAINER may call to me as a challenge. An interesting or treasured container is the perfect inspiration for gathering and arranging flowers to compliment something of value.

The OCCASION may be the motivator of creativity. When I am sharing emotions with others, the language of flowers helps me to congratulate, sympathize, love, or portray the ways I care for others.

I don't need a lot of "natural" artistic ability to arrange flowers. I only need the desire and the motivation. The flowers, the container, and/or the occasion will do their part to create beauty.

My privilege in flower arranging is to *enjoy the process!*

· O ·

You Rescue Me!

My Dear Lord,

I have pondered to understand, and I go into a quiet place to be with You. But, when my heart is bitter, I am senseless and ignorant.

You, Lord, have taken my right hand and guided me with Your wisdom and Your counsel. Whom have I in heaven but You, Lord? I desire no one on earth as much as I desire You. (Oh, what a lifelong surrendering to come to this point!)

I will get as close to You, Lord, as I can, for when I draw near to You, You draw near to me. And, the nearness of You is my good. Lord, I have made You my refuge. I have chosen You, and I will tell of the wonderful ways *You rescue me!*

· O ·

—Psalm 73, Isaiah 41, and James 4 [paraphrase mine]

It Took Death To Come Alive

My Dear Lord,

I remember the Easter Morning I awoke very early and sat quietly in my reading chair enjoying the non-sounds of early morning. I stared out the window while visions of Your death became very vivid to me.

I could see You hanging on the cross with blood and tears and pain on Your face. I wondered why You were required to suffer, and I also wondered why I was suffering, too. Then, the words came clearly to me: "It Took Death To Come Alive."

As clearly as I would have heard my child calling in the middle of the night, I heard You say: "Go and find the poem!" I knew immediately which poem You meant.

When my son was only nine years old, he was
studying the life of Vincent Van Gogh and had written
a haiku about Van Gogh's life. I knew the poem was
profound at the time, but I had no idea the impact
that my small child's writing would have on my life.
Bill wrote:

> Now, we understand
> It took death to come alive
> Not during his time

In those quiet moments that Easter Morning, You
said to me: "Here's your message, Rita. Run this
thread through all your art: I have given you
the art of writing and drawing and flower
arranging to communicate My message—
it took death to come alive.

· O ·

Rita

Just Awesome!

My Dear Lord,

I attempted an oil painting class this summer, and You know the frustration I experienced. I worked in class with some degree of confidence and took the teacher's remarks as constructive. Some classes seemed more productive than others, and, all in all, I was encouraged.

I came home from my final class and proudly stood my two oil paintings against a wall in the kitchen so I could view them in a different setting with new light.

A family member walked through the kitchen, took one quick look, and casually remarked: "Gotta long way to go, don't you?" Painful, but true, I really do have a long way to go.

There are two kinds of critics: ones who offer advice without solutions and ones who offer advice with solutions.

Help me to weather both these critics and allow me to be just awful on the way to becoming *just awesome.*

· O ·

The life which is not examined is not worth living.
—Plato

Mine Time

My Dear Lord,

Finding a time that's mine
is
truly a selfish act
but
it's the necessary focus on self
that
makes me
fit
for anyone else.

Lord, children are not taught the word "mine," they
just seem to instinctively know it when someone
threatens to take away their possessions.

Teach me to guard the time I spend with You each
day with a healthy dose of childlike possessiveness.

I love *mine time* with You!

· O ·

Not Just a Taker

My Dear Lord,

Thank you for the words
I needed to hear today:
"My child, evaluate
your energies and
how you use them."
(*The Fruit of the
Spirit*, Sarah
Hornsby)

This is a
powerful
request from
You, Lord, as I
discover the
great amounts of time
and energy that I spend on things
rather than people. Your gift to me
is people. How
wrong I am to
concentrate on
"things" of this
world rather
than the
precious
people of
Your creation.

People need Encouragement,
People need Healing,
People need Rest.

Teach me, Lord,
to be a giver
in this world and
not just a taker.

· O ·

The Next Fifty Years

My Dear Lord,

It's taken three mothers to raise me. And as I approach the age of fifty, I'm just now beginning to feel "grown up."

There have been three mothers in my life: Grandmother Johnson, Great-mama Elizabeth, and my mother Sue, who are all a part of who I am.

Grandmother Johnson taught me: "Never Give Up!"

Great-mama Elizabeth taught me: "Insist On The Best And Never Take Less!"

Mother Sue taught me: "Anything Is Possible!"

What a dynamic recipe for mothering!

Perseverance
and
Persistence
and
Encouragement

Dear Lord, please
let my three mothers'
virtues guide me
as I continue to
grow up in
the next fifty years!

· O ·

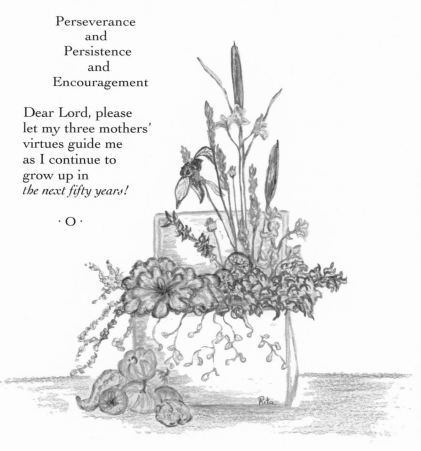

Lines of Confusion

My Dear Lord,

There is a design style in flower arranging called "Lines of Confusion," and it takes a pretty good designer to pull this one off without it looking like a mess. But, I love the description, "Lines of Confusion."

I see this as the perfect description of the roadblocks I have set up for myself to stymie my creative dreams.

To all the lines of confusion I erect, the answer is the same. Never.
Or, probably never.

Therefore, the now-popular phrase
"Get over it!"
seems very
appropriate.

My "Lines of Confusion" are:
—when my children don't need me;
  —when I get proficient at the computer;
  —when I learn to spell better;
  —when I have a workroom to call
    my own;
    —when I have read enough;
    —when I am no longer criticized;
      —etc., etc., etc., etc., etc.

Thank you, dear Lord, for
  helping me "get over"
    my *lines of confusion*.

· O ·

Grand and Magnificent

My Dear Lord,

Here "In The Growing Places,"
I have no greater prayer
than that the words I speak
and the thoughts I think
will be pleasing to You.

Your goodness to me is beyond description.
What a small offering I bring to You
of words and thoughts,
but,
When they are Your words
and Your thoughts,
they are truly
grand and magnificent!

· O ·

May my spoken words and unspoken thoughts
be pleasing even to you, O Lord my Rock
and my Redeemer.
—Psalm 19:14 TLB

Hiding in the Dirt

My Dear Lord,

There's a Prayer Patch out there
hiding in the dirt!
Dig in.
It's okay to get your
fingernails dirty
and fall to your knees,
digging in the dirt.

God is also there
in the dirt.
You see His beauty
in the glorious
colors
and shapes
of growing things.

You feel His rest
in the coolness of
the earth
as you dig
beneath
the top layer of
soil.

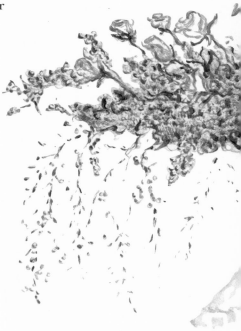

You touch His strength
in the sturdy stems
that carry nourishment
throughout the plant.

You hear His voice
in the gentle sound
of the wind
and of the rain.

Draw me into Your
Prayer Patch, Lord,
and remind me
that it is readily
available in my
time of need.
Draw me into Your
Prayer Patch, Lord,
into Your Glories
which are out there
hiding in the dirt!

· O ·

He Sucks His Thumb

My Dear Lord,

He looks at me sweetly and says,
"Up here, up here."

He climbs on my lap,
a feeling so dear.

And then comes the moment
I'll never replace

When
he sucks his thumb
and touches my face!

· O ·

*Stephen, who gave me this moment, is now a young man and
is still giving me moments I'll never replace.*

My Own Uniqueness

My Dear Lord,

For years, I thought that one more art class or one more teacher would be the answer to the insecurity I felt about my drawing ability. All of my formal art experiences led to frustration, for I was being told to "draw larger, use bigger brushes, use more color, be loose with the paint."

Soon, I discovered that some artists see smaller than life! What a relief to accept that as my unique style! Now, I am content to create in my own way. What joy comes from an acceptance of *my own uniqueness!*

· O ·

One of the characteristics of great drawings is the artist's
wholehearted acceptance of his own style and character. It is as
if the drawing says for the artist: "Here I am!"
—Nathan Goldstein

Hope Through Creativity

My Dear Lord,

You tell me in Your Word that "all things work together for good" for those who love You. I love You, Lord. But, in the midst of my pain there seems to be very little working together for good. How do I find where the pain ends and the creativity begins?

I trust you now, Lord, as I dip into your deep well of creative thoughts, creative solutions, and creative deeds.

I love you, Lord, for giving me *hope through creativity!*

· O ·

The Tight-Lipped Woman

My Dear Lord,

"Beware of the tight-lipped woman. She has been mad at someone for a very long time."

You know how easy and how much fun it is to hold grudges. We allow ourselves the luxury of hatred and self-righteousness. If only we could see ourselves as the years take control of our faces and turn them into mirrors of our anger.

Dear Lord, You can loosen the muscles, You can release the tension, and You can turn me from *the tight-lipped woman* into a woman with praise on my lips.

· O ·

As in water face reflects face.
—Proverbs 27:19

The Person You Would Have Me Be

My Dear Lord,

Every day I must
take a walk
with You
either through my garden of flowers and foliage
or
through the words written in my journal
or
through the images made by my drawings.

These walks with You, Lord,
are as necessary
as the
air I breathe
or
the water I drink,
for it is during these walks, Lord,
that You nurture me
and
create in me
the person you would have me be.

· O ·

A passion in life will keep you alive. The wonderful thing about flower arranging is that there is always something to learn.
—*Marlin Phythyon*

Say What I Need To Hear

My Dear Lord,

I've learned a trick that works wonders when I need a compliment. I *say* to someone else what I need to hear! For example, I may need to hear:

"You look nice today!"
"I'm proud of you!"
"You're always so generous!"
"I love you!"
"It's great that you never give up!"
"Thanks for caring!"

So, when I need to hear these words, I *say* these words of encouragement out loud. Then, two people are happy—the Giver and the Receiver. Thank you, Lord, for this simple way you've taught me to *say what I need to hear!*

· O ·

he Old Mama

My Dear Lord,

My children have had to
"make room for Mama."

In the early years of my flower arranging, our oldest son
walked into the kitchen one day and found every inch of
counter space covered with flowers and leaves
and buckets.
He stayed just long enough to realize there was nothing
to eat and no real prospect of food any time soon.

Brad said, "You know, Mama, some mothers cook in
their kitchens!" With a dramatic flip of my hair, I
replied: "That was *the old Mama!*"

· O ·

In the Morning

My Dear Lord,

I meet you here in the morning, Lord,
when all is quiet
and the only one needing me is
You.

I meet you here in the morning, Lord,
it's my favorite time of day.
I sit,
I think,
I listen,
I pray.

I meet you here in the morning, Lord,
when your voice is clear
and
when my mind is not yet cluttered
with the sights and sounds
that come with the sun.

I meet you here *in the morning*, Lord,
like two lovers we rendezvous,
each with our gifts for the other,
each with the hope
of a life made
new.

· O ·

Early will I seek thee.
—Psalm 5:3
[paraphrase mine]

Your Name Is "Providence"

My Dear Lord,

I've seen providence happen! There is no way that I could have orchestrated or manipulated some of the people and places that have presented themselves to me without Your divine intervention.

Lord, when I take a step in Your direction, the doors open and I know that it could only be You standing there opening the door.

In the *Scottish Himalayan Expedition*, W. H. Murray says: "the moment one definitely commits oneself, then Providence moves, too."

My dear Lord, *Your name is "Providence!"*

· O ·

Flower Arranging Recipes

The "recipes" are very brief because it is my belief that flower arranging should be fun and easy. Here you will find some further explanation of terms and instructions.

Floral foam: A highly absorbent material used to hold plant material in place and supply a water source.

Fruits and vegetables: Secure with picks. Wooden floral picks or bamboo skewers can be used to secure fruits and vegetables by placing the pointed end into the fruit and the other end positioned into the floral foam.

Kenzan: A needlepoint holder used in oriental floral design. Flowers and foliage are placed directly onto the sharp needle points.

Mechanics: Any method or device used to construct a flower arrangement.

Moss: Used to cover mechanics at the base of a design. Moss can be secured into the foam with a u-shaped pin or wire.

Plastic dish placed at lip of container: The design is built into a dish which can be secured to the lip of a container with floral clay.

Taped-in floral foam: Use a waterproof floral tape to secure the foam into a liner. Taping across and around the foam in two directions adds to its security.

Vase inside a vase: An inexpensive vase or cup placed inside a valuable container is a good idea to protect your container.

Waterproof tape: An essential tool in flower arranging; comes in clear or green tape.

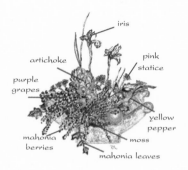

artichoke

iris

purple grapes

pink statice

mahonia berries

yellow pepper

moss

mahonia leaves

Calling My Name
pages 2-3
Vegetables, fruits, and flowers are quite comfortable in this antique cheese cradle. Floral foam is taped into plastic liner; fruits and vegetables are secured with picks.

Encourager and Critic
pages 4-5
The ceramic cylinder is filled with floral foam cut to fit tightly so that the sides of the vase secure the flowers and foliage. The tropicals used together are dramatic.
Original design by Joseph E. Smith

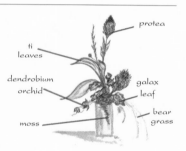

protea

ti leaves

dendrobium orchid

galax leaf

bear grass

moss

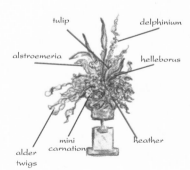

tulip

delphinium

alstroemeria

helleborus

mini carnation

heather

alder twigs

Something Beautiful for God
pages 6-7
A pair of urns should look similiar but never exactly alike and should draw attention to the object placed between them. Floral foam is taped into plastic liners.
Original design by Sheila Macqueen

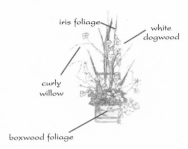

iris foliage

white dogwood

curly willow

boxwood foliage

Only After
pages 8-9
A wooden basket is the perfect container for the natural look of dogwood branches. Floral foam is taped into a plastic dish which fits inside the basket.

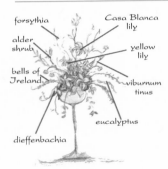

forsythia

alder shrub

bells of Ireland

dieffenbachia

Casa Blanca lily

yellow lily

viburnum tinus

eucalyptus

Really Me
pages 10-11
A large pedestal is required for this mass design. Secure very well the floral foam inside the vase liner and place it deeply inside so that the sides of the container help to support the plant material.
Original design by Sheila Macqueen

Moment in Time
page 12
All mechanics are covered in this design by using a shallow dish filled with floral foam and secured with tape. Flowers and foliage cover the base. Moss is used to give an earthy feel.

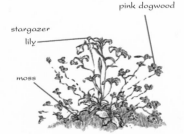

pink dogwood

stargazer lily

moss

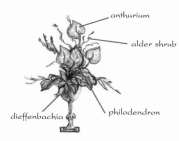

anthurium
alder shrub
dieffenbachia
philodendron

You and Me, Lord
page 13
An alabaster vase compliments the color of the anthuriums. The simple mechanics are floral foam placed inside the alabaster vase.
Original design by Sheila Macqueen

The Trash Before the Treasure
pages 14-15
A tall cylinder vase is the foundation of this design. Your eye is carried from top to bottom by placing a small container with flowers at the base. Floral foam is placed inside the cylinder and the small container.

gerbera daisy
eucalyptus
eucalyptus
bear grass

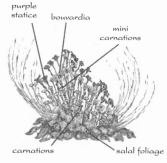

purple statice
bouvardia
mini carnations
carnations
salal foliage

Your Joy May Be Made Full
pages 16-17
A shallow fifteen-inch-diameter circular dish is used to support this large design which can be viewed from all sides. Cut floral foam to fill the dish and secure with tape; leave about one inch of foam above the lip of the container for easy insertion of flowers and foliage.

Belonging to You
page 18

This copper oriental urn elevates the design to allow a lovely balance. A plastic liner is used to hold flowers. Tape floral foam into liner.

Original design by Shelia Macqueen

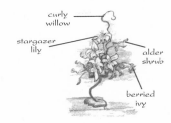

curly willow

stargazer lily

alder shrub

berried ivy

An Empty Person
page 19

A single heliconia bloom is all that's needed to make a bold statement. The tulips at the base are reflexed to see the beauty inside. All plant material is placed in a shallow round dish filled with taped-in floral foam.

Original design by Joseph E. Smith

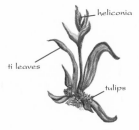

heliconia

ti leaves

tulips

Pray Before I Speak
pages 20-21

A long rectangular container supports this linear design. The floral foam is placed into the container with one inch of foam above the lip. Tape the foam with a continuous motion as if wrapping around, leaving 3–4 inches between the tape.

Painting by Paul Harmon

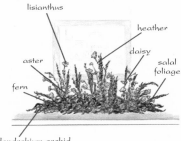

lisianthus

heather

daisy

aster

salal foliage

fern

dendrobium orchid

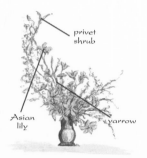

privet
shrub

Asian
lily

yarrow

The Interruptions
pages 22-23
A heavy pewter vase is used here with an oversized design to add drama. The floral foam is put directly into the vase and fills the entire vase.

Manually Competent
pages 24-25
The plant material and vase are in perfect harmony in this Ikebana design. A kenzan (needlepoint holder) is used to secure all materials.
Original design by Martha Kesler

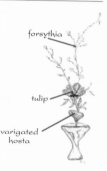

forsythia

tulip

varigated
hosta

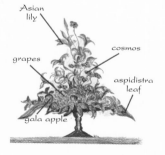

Asian
lily

cosmos

grapes

aspidistra
leaf

gala apple

In Silence
pages 26-27
The bowl to this wooden compote is an elongated oval which lends itself very well to the base of this triangular design. Floral foam is taped into a plastic liner.

Listening Is Learning
pages 28-29
This beautifully shaped tall clear glass vase is filled with water, and the floral design is placed into the top opening. Design flowers in a bowl with taped-in floral foam.

delphinium

daisy

misty blue statice

snapdragon

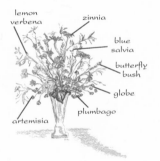

lemon verbena

zinnia

blue salvia

butterfly bush

globe

plumbago

artemisia

Work of Art
pages 30-31
The floral foam is cut to fit and placed directly into this repaired blue vase. The un-arranged look of these garden flowers sweeten its charm.

Enjoy the Process
pages 32-33
Zinnias with their heavy foliage, and salvia are arranged easily in this fired-clay pot. The small wooden vases are filled with water. The big pot is elevated by a wood slice from a cut tree, and all elements are placed on a wooden tray.

zinnia leaves

zinnia

blue salvia

cosmos

You Rescue Me!
pages 34-35
In the garden, cosmos will attract
hundreds of butterflies. What could be
more joyful than a bunch of cosmos
loosely placed in a glass container?
Crisscross the stems to give the
arrangement stability.

It Took Death To Come Alive
pages 36-37
Floral foam is taped into a plastic liner
and set into the basket. For this design
an old basket has been covered with
sheet moss by hot gluing the moss onto
all the surfaces. Flowers are placed
casually around the handle.

gerbera

dusty
miller
foliage

dusty
miller
bloom

rose

hedge
apples

caladium

hosta leaves

purple
cone flower

ornamental
zebra grass

Just Awesome!
pages 38-39
The large glass vase is filled with water,
and the design is constructed in a bowl
which fits into the lip of the container.
Floral foam is taped securely into a
clear glass bowl.

Mine Time
pages 40-41
This clear glass cylinder has been filled
with a substance called "California
Crystals™." These crystals expand in
water and feel like clear gelatin. It gives
great support to plant material and looks
like crushed ice.

tulip

kiwi vine

lily grass

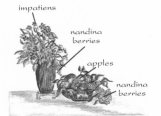

impatiens

nandina berries

apples

nandina berries

Not Just a Taker
pages 42-43
These mature impatiens with long
stems were placed directly into the
vase of water, crisscrossing stems for
support. The bowl of fruits and
berries is arranged without the need
of a water source.

The Next Fifty Years
pages 44-45
A plastic pan was found that fit
perfectly into the lip of the basket.
The pan was filled with floral foam
and raised to the correct level with
crumpled newspaper. Fruits and
vegetables were secured with
floral picks.

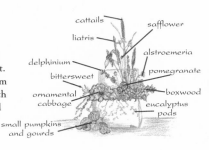

cattails

safflower

liatris

alstroemeria

delphinium

bittersweet

pomegranate

ornamental cabbage

boxwood

eucalyptus pods

small pumpkins and gourds

curly willow

gladiolus

Lines of Confusion
pages 46-47
The plant material in this
Ikebana arrangement is
supported by the design of the
container which is filled with
water.
Original design by Martha Kesler

Grand and Magnificent
pages 48-49
The contemporary look of this copper
container makes it a favorite. The copper
bowl is protected with a plastic liner.
Floral foam is taped into the liner.

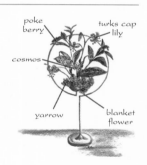

poke
berry

turks cap
lily

cosmos

yarrow

blanket
flower

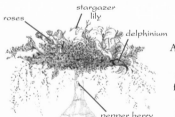

roses

stargazer
lily

delphinium

pepper berry

Hiding in the Dirt
pages 50-51
A clear glass cake stand is used as the
base for this design. The flowers,
foliage, and berries are arranged to
fill a circular shallow dish which fits
the flat surface on the stand. Floral
foam is taped into the shallow dish.

He Sucks His Thumb
pages 52-53
This container is an American Indian
fired-clay pot into which floral foam
has been cut to fit. The background
is a primitive art screen.

cattail

gerbera

bittersweet

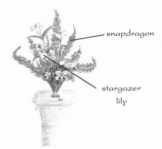

snapdragon

stargazer
lily

My Own Uniqueness
pages 54-55
Snapdragons form a frame for the
lilies which point to the center. The
design is in a fan-shaped vase filled
with floral foam cut to fit.

Hope Through Creativity
pages 56-57
A shallow six-inch round plastic dish
is the base of this design. Floral
foam has been taped into the dish,
and all mechanics are covered with
plant material.

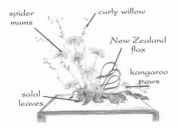

spider
mums

curly willow

New Zealand
flax

kangaroo
paws

salal
leaves

bird of
paradise

daisy
mum

liatris

gerbera

china
aster

nandina
berries

The Tight-Lipped Woman
pages 58-59

The woman's face is painted onto a
pumpkin. An opening is cut in the top
of the pumpkin just big enough for a
round plastic dish with taped-in floral
foam. The top of a straw hat was cut
out, and the brim placed between the
flowers and the pumpkin. What fun!

Face painted by Mary Claire Shrewsbury

The Person You Would Have Me Be
pages 60-61

Old-fashioned roses are noted
for their lovely scent and
long-flowering season.

old-fashioned climbing rose

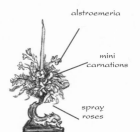

alstroemeria

mini
carnations

spray
roses

Say What I Need To Hear
pages 62-63

The bowl of this dolphin vase is
protected with a metal liner (an English
cupholder) and filled with floral foam
secured with tape. The candle is placed
directly into the center of the flowers.

Original design by Sheila Macqueen

The Old Mama
pages 64-65

A wooden tray supports the clay house made in my son's art class. A small dish (with taped-in floral foam) of plant material is opposite the clay house. Flowers coming out of the house are placed into a cup of taped-in floral foam. Moss is used around the house to give it the natural look of a landscape design.

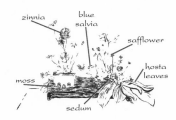

In the Morning
pages 66-67

A clear glass outer vase is lined with a clear glass cylinder vase which supports the plant material in water. The double glass is an unusual and interesting effect.

Your Name Is "Providence"
pages 68-69

The large marble urn is filled with floral foam cut to fit snugly so that the sides of the urn aid in support of the plant material. The curly willow pointing to the urn is a beautiful technique.

Original design by Sheila Macqueen

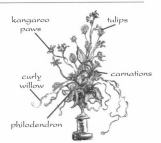